Instagram Evolution

The Ultimate Guide to Grow Your Brand from Zero to Hero in 2021

Michael Kouiroukidis

Special thanks to my dear editor

Copyright © 2020 by Michael Kouiroukidis
Self-published
Michael.kouiroukidis@web.de

All rights reserved.
No part of this publication may be reproduced, stored in a retrieval system, stored in a database and / or published in any form or by any means, electronic, mechanical, photocopying, recording or otherwise, without the prior written permission of the publisher except for the quotation of the book.

Table of Contents

1. Introduction...4
2. Establishing the Foundations 6
   2.1 Bring Your Profile to Perfection 7
3. Engaging with Other People (Follow for Follow) 9
   3.1 Identifying target accounts..10
   3.2 Following...11
   3.3 Unfollowing 15
   3.4 Conclusion for The Follow for Follow Method.................16
4. Engagement Groups 17
   4.1 Understanding How Engagement Helps Your Posts........17
   4.2 Likes from Larger Accounts Count More Than Those from Smaller Accounts...18
   4.3 Create Your Own Engagement Group..............................18
   4.4 Set Your Rules...19
   4.5 Conclusion Engagement Groups......................................20
5. Shoutouts 21
   5.1 Detecting a Good Profile...21
   5.2 Shoutout for Shoutout...22
   5.3 Paid Shoutouts 22
   5.4 Conclusion Shoutouts...23
6. The Viral Comment Method 24
   6.1 How it Works...24
   6.2 Conclusion to The Viral Comment Method 25
7. Improve Your Engagement Rate...26
   7.1 Do Not Post Too Often 26
   7.2 Be Consistent 27

7.3 Engage with Your Followers 27
7.4 Post Engaging Captions 28
7.5 Remove Bot Followers... 28
8. The Correct use of Hashtags 29
　8.1 How to Do Hashtag Research 30
　8.2 Create Your Own Hashtag.. 35
9. Account Trust Score.. 35
　9.1 What Happens if Your Account Trust Score is Bad?........ 39
10. Use Other Social Media Platforms (Reddit) 39
　10.1 Finding the Right Subreddit 40
　10.2 Get Yourself Familiar with The Rules 40
　10.3 Things to Consider When Posting 41
　10.4 Conclusion on Social Media Platforms (Reddit) 42
11. Summing Up... 43
12. Did You Enjoy Reading This Book? 45

1. Introduction

Growing on Instagram for people that are not well known to the world seems to be nearly impossible nowadays. Countless Instagram users head online every day, being fully motivated and putting hard work into creating amazing content to post online in the hopes of becoming an Instagram influencer and their dream to start earning money with their hobbies. However, most of them fail and never even make it past 1.000 followers. As a result, many friends have asked me this before: "How on earth do you grow on Instagram?". You might have asked the same question before without coming to a conclusion but this book will finally give you straight answers on how you can grow your Instagram account, whether it is about your business, your hobby or your dog. If you have not noticed it before then this will be your very first lesson: Growing your account from scratch by simply posting pictures is impossible!

Instagram Growth can be compared to launching a spacecraft. In the initial phase (launch phase) you will need an extreme amount of energy to lift off the ground and start getting more followers (reaching space). The higher up you are, the less energy you will need to keep going. Once you leave the orbit, the craft flies by itself and does not need much additional power to keep going as there are not many particles that can slow it down. This analogy is very helpful to understand what it takes to grow on Instagram and shows just how hard the first stage really is. However, it also shows that it gets easier and easier the further you go.

In order to grow your account from zero to hero, you will need to put in hard work and use methods and techniques that will bring you active followers which will allow you to push your content out to the world and more importantly, to the explore page of Instagram. Real growth means more than just having a high number of followers. It all comes down to how active and how engaged those followers are with your content as they will mean nothing if they never interact with your content and if they have no interest in your posts. The methods that will actually help your account grow will be introduced and explained in detail in the course of this book and I will guide you through the different steps that will lead you to build up your successful Instagram account. If you hang on until the end and read through the whole book you will be rewarded as I will share my favourite and strongest method for growing in the end.

I have worked with multiple small businesses, influencers and organizations and helped them grow their followers and fanbase for a substantial amount. These methods have all been field tested to ensure that you can grow your account too using the methods explained in this book. Furthermore, I have created a subreddit (reddit.com/r/InstagramEvolution) around this book where you can ask questions related to social media marketing, share your experiences or connect to like-minded people. You can follow my journey on my personal Instagram account: @michael_kalamaris which is mainly photography related.

2. Establishing the Foundations

There are many methods to help you grow your Instagram account, such as the proper use of Hashtags, Shoutouts for Shoutouts, Engagement groups and more. Most of them, however, require you to have a decent amount of followers to be effective in growing your account, thus you might think what do you do if you are just starting out and have less than a thousand followers? The answer is rather simple, you need to engage with other Instagram users to make them aware of your account, get them to check out your profile and potentially follow you if they like it. This is a great way to reach others since you won't be able to rank in the top posts of a hashtag because your posts do not get enough likes and comments. When doing this, all that matters is your profile quality and the fact that you are genuine when you engage with other people's profiles. Don't be too spammy, leave real comments and like pictures that are within your own niche to make the most of your time. **Very important**: stay away from fake followers or fake likes! Instagram is a marathon, not a sprint. If you try to artificially grow your account by buying followers all you do is hurt your Instagram account. Many panels will offer you "real followers" for money, but the truth is, that they are 100% bot accounts that will never ever engage with your content again and hurt your account trust score (more to that later). Hence, you need to use strategies that *organically* grow your account without having to use methods that hurt your account in the long run. "Organically" or "organic growth" are terms used to describe a process that does not rely on automation or other bot actions and grows an account naturally with the tools provided by Instagram itself (no gene manipulation).

2.1 Bring Your Profile to Perfection

The first part might not be the most thrilling topic, however, it is actually very important to have an authentic and good profile. More importantly, is that there are many hidden features when it comes to your profile that play a role in your account trust score which eventually correlates to your growth on Instagram. Furthermore, we will take a look at ways to make your profile more compelling for others to want to look through it and follow you.

Business/Creator vs Personal Account

The first challenge already arises when you need to think about whether to have a business/creator or a personal account. The benefits of switching to a business or creator account are that you can add a contact button but more importantly that you gain access to analytics that show you where your posts were seen the most, when your followers are the most active and much more.

The screenshot above is taken from one of my accounts that only had 700 followers at that time. As you can see this information can be very helpful to determine if you post made it to the top hashtags. This post was seen by almost 11.000 people just by ranking well in the hashtags, it was shared very often and many people saved the image. This tells me that the post was successful and I can now try to mimic that one for future posts. Moreover, if you have a creator account you can access your insights on the creator studio page on Facebook. I have often read that switching to a business profile is limiting the reach of the account and the posts get less engagement. However, I do not believe this to be true since I have never experienced the same phenomenon and never seen any real studies that prove that. Furthermore, a look at large Instagram accounts will show that many of them use a business or creator profile, so I truly believe that getting a business or a creator account is beneficial for growing your account.

Have an Engaging and Real Looking Profile and Bio:
This might be the most obvious one of them all so I will keep it short. Your Account should awaken the interest of the person that is viewing your account. But the most important aspect of your account is that it needs to look *real* and original. If you account looks unfinished or messy then you might be seen as a bot by many users and they will not follow you even if your posts are great. Instagram is a social media platform after all, and people want to connect to real people and not some programmed bot that works by itself. Try to be unique and ask your friends what they think about your bio, oftentimes you might get valuable feedback.

3. Engaging with Other People (Follow for Follow)

Now let us get to the first method for actually gaining new followers. The Follow for Follow or Follow/Unfollow method is probably the most known and commonly used method to grow on Instagram. However, it can leave a negative mark for your brand/profile page because of its nature to unfollow people, at least those who do not follow you back, after a certain amount of time again. Yet, it is extremely efficient in gaining your first few followers. As a small account you will struggle getting your posts seen by other users so you will need to get traction elsewhere. One simple and fast way of doing it is by following users within the same niche as yours with the goal to get them to follow you back. After you follow a person on Instagram, they receive a notification that you just followed them. Most users consequently check out your profile as they are interested to see who the new follower is. If they notice that you share the same interests as they do, chances are high that they will follow you back as a sign of gratitude and solidarity. After all, we are all in the same boat.

By using the Follow/Unfollow method, you will gain followers that are high quality, they have the same interest as you since you can target those directly and because you share the same interests they are very likely to engage with your future content. These are all things that are very important for account growth as you will need to have an excellent **engagement rate** in order to continue and skyrocket your growth on Instagram. Your engagement rate is the percentage (%) of people that engage with your content relative to the total amount of your followers, the higher this percentage (%) the better. If you follow the steps below, you will gain a lot of new followers while keeping your engagement rate high. The first step in the Follow for Follow method is to find accounts that you want to interact with and that are within your field of interest (niche). One simple way of doing this is to look for larger accounts (targets) within your niche but make sure that those accounts are not too big (i.e. no celebrity accounts).

3.1 Identifying target accounts

You can find potential target accounts by searching through the "top posts" of a hashtag that is within your niche. Browse through the top posts and check out the profiles of those posts, if they are big enough you can further investigate. Your target accounts should be accounts with a good engagement rate. You can use websites like igblade.com to get statistics on an account and with the help of those statistics you can determine if the account in question is a good target to use for your Follow/Unfollow method. Ideally, you should look for accounts that have more than 10.000 followers and less than 100.000 followers with an average engagement rate of more than 5%. Look at their comments and see if they are genuine and real comments, if their comments are mostly emojis or out of context then you should look for another target since the followers might likely be bot accounts.

These values are important to rule out any accounts that have inactive or bot followers. Furthermore, celebrity accounts have a very dedicated fan base that is only interested in their content and thus less likely to follow you back. As you might have noticed, bots are a real plague on Instagram, and you will often come across accounts that have thousands of followers but only a few likes on their posts. Therefore, it is not the number of followers you should mainly be looking at but the quality of those, which you can easily detect when you look at the engagement rate and the authenticity of their comments. The main goal for you is to not only gain new followers, but gain followers that engage with your content, like your new posts and post comments or share it with their friends.

3.2 Following

Now that you determined a target you can go to their latest post and look through the people that liked that picture. Look for accounts that have a profile picture, an authentic name (not something like hot_babes133) and are personal accounts (no brand accounts) that have less than 2.000 followers. Brand accounts might follow you back but are usually not likely to like or comment on your posts, they are focused more around their own content and brand so you should try to avoid them first. Furthermore, accounts that you want to follow should have a good following-to-followers ratio which means that they should be following a good amount of people relative to their number of followers. Here is a good example of an account that is very likely to follow you back once you followed them:

As you can see the account looks really authentic, they have a lot of posts which indicates an active profile and a followers-to-following ratio of almost 1:1 which indicates a really high success in them following you back once you followed them as long as you are within the same niche (in this scenario photography/nature). The goal is to get the highest follow-back ratio out of those accounts that you follow, so you won't have to unfollow as many people as a result (you will need to unfollow those who don't follow you back at some point). After you follow a person, make sure to go into their profile and select 2 pictures and like them. It is important that you do not just like the 2 most recent pictures but choose one that is a little older so (example shown below) that the person knows that you have actually looked through their profile and not just quickly liked 2 posts and left.

Furthermore, if you really like the profile, you can comment on one of their pictures with a genuine and individual comment to higher the chances of receiving a follow-back from that person. Posting real comments in combination with liking 2 different pictures will separate you from the masses that use the Follow for Follow method as most users just spam follow in the hopes to quickly grow their accounts without putting real effort into it.

If you use this method correctly then you will be able to achieve a follow-back ratio around 30-40%. This means for every 100 accounts that you follow, you will receive around 30-40 followers. This number depends on the niche and the quality of your posts and your profile page. Therefore, you can get up to 80 followers a day which equals 560 followers per week or 2480 followers each month. Admittedly, these numbers are a little ambitious especially for someone who does not have experience in growing an account yet so I will provide a table with growth projections for an average user who uses this method.

Below you can find a prediction with a Follow-Back ratio of

Day	Following	Followers Gained	Total
1	+200	+20	20
2	+200	+20	40
3	+200	+40	80
4	+200	+40	120
5	+200	+60	180
6	+200	+60	240
7	+200	+60	300
...	...	...	...
30	+200	+60	1680

30% Since the first few followers are the hardest, I calculated a follow-back ratio of 10% for the first 2 days. Afterwards you will be getting around 20% which will equal a total of 40 followers per day. Eventually, you will hit the 30% follow-back ratio which is very realistic to get after you have more than 100 followers which occurs after the 4th day. As you can see, reaching more than 1.000 followers in your first month is very realistic and you can definitely achieve it via the Follow/Unfollow method, but I recommend that you do not overuse it.

Follow Limits

Instagram is much more rigorous than it used to be. Based on my experience over the past few months you should limit your actions to around 200 follows and 400 likes with an additional 200 unfollows per day is unproblematic as long as you do it all manually without the help of automation. If you want to be completely safe you can limit your actions to 150 follows/unfollows and 300 likes per day. You always need to consider different things when you look at limits such as account age, previous infractions or blocks, timeframe of the actions. Generally speaking, make sure to not exercise any spammy behaviour whenever you are active on Instagram, spread your actions throughout the day and do not follow more than 100 people in one hour, otherwise you will quickly get action blocks which will stop you from doing anything on Instagram for a certain period of time.

3.3 Unfollowing

Unfortunately, the unfollowing is the ugly but necessary part in this method that needs to be done. If you are following significantly more accounts than accounts are following you, then your account will end up looking unauthentic and spammy. People will immediately see that you use the method of following people in the hopes of getting a follow back which will make them much less likely to follow you back once you follow them. You can think of your following (the accounts that you follow) as some sort of worth that decreases the more people you are followed to. If someone checks out your account and sees that you are following 5.000 other people, then the person will not see himself as "special". They are just one of 5.000 and might end up being annoyed instead of flattered since they can easily see what you are trying to do and what your motivations really are. Hence, it is crucial to keep the number of accounts that you are followed to lower than the followers that you have. To do this efficiently, only unfollow those who do not follow you back after one day of following them. You can get tools to identify those who aren't followed to you and then you can go through the list and unfollow them manually. Even though there are often apps i.e. "followers cleaner" that are used to mass unfollow again, I would recommend that you only use the apps to scrape (search through) those who have not followed you back and then manually unfollow them otherwise your account will most likely be hit by an action limit, shadow ban or worse. Once your account becomes larger and you stop the Follow/Unfollow method you can decide if you want to unfollow those accounts that have followed you back. This depends on how much you want to "bond" with your followers as they will be negatively impacted if you unfollow them. Furthermore, by only unfollowing those who did not follow you back you avoid being reported as spam by many people since they might not even notice that you followed and unfollowed them.

Consumer vs. Creator

Instagram hiddenly ranks users in many different ways and one of them is to rank them as either a consumer or a content creator. If you are following many people you will be put in the consumer category which is programmed to offer you the best user experience and help you find more content that you like. The issue, however, is that your posts will be handicapped as they will not reach the explore page and rank worse in hashtags since Instagram does not view you as a good account to be put into the explore page. Thus, it is recommended to keep the number of followed users to below 500 and in the best scenario below 100.

3.4 Conclusion for The Follow for Follow Method

The Follow for Follow method is great to give you a kickstart and a fair chance on your Instagram growth project but it is a double-edged sword. You need to be careful to not exercise too spammy behaviours and you need to stop doing it before it is too late. If you only use the Follow for Follow method, you will eventually end up completely depending on it to grow at all because your reach will be limited and you will not be able to naturally gain further followers. If you are not cautious you will end up putting too much weight on the spacecraft and it will never be able to leave orbit and be on a free flight. As a result, I recommend using this method until you reach around 1.000 followers and then you will have enough options to go for without using the Follow for Follow method any longer or only occasionally.

4. Engagement Groups

Engagement groups can be a real boost to your growth, but they are only really worth it once you have reached more than 1.000 followers because they work best with slightly bigger accounts. Engagement groups are group chats that consist of people that have accounts within the same niche for example: photography. The people in there like and comment on each other's new posts in order to raise the engagement and have it rank higher in hashtags and provide a better chance to reach the explore page. Those engagement groups vary a lot in size and quality so it is very important that you understand how these work exactly and why they can help out your account growth.

4.1 Understanding How Engagement Helps Your Posts

You probably already know that your posts are seen by more people the more likes and comments it has. If your post is seen by 1.000 people but only 100 of them like the post and nobody leaves a comment then this is an indicator for Instagram that this post is terrible and they will limit its reach severely and you will have no chance to rank in hashtags. But if your account is seen by 1.000 people and gets more than 600 likes and 50 comments then this is a great indicator that your content is amazing. Instagram realizes that your content is amazing, so they push it out for other people to see it as well, thus it ranks high in hashtags and has a chance to be seen in the explore page. The most crucial time frame for this ranking are the first 1-2 hours of your post. If it gets a lot of engagement in that time frame, then you have higher chances of ranking as a top post in hashtags and be seen in the explore page.

BUT: Not all engagement is good. If you get a lot of likes from low quality accounts such as bots or spam accounts, then this will actually hurt your chances of ranking high and your post will be limited. Therefore, it is necessary to only take part in engagement groups with exclusively high quality accounts. Stay away from large engagement groups that have hundreds of users and make sure to quality check the accounts before you start being an active part in an engagement group.

4.2 Likes from Larger Accounts Count More Than Those from Smaller Accounts

This part is why it does not make much sense to be in engagement groups before you reach a thousand followers. Likes from larger accounts count more than those from smaller accounts. Larger accounts simply have more value to Instagram, and they have a higher authority than a small account because they have proven themselves to be vital parts of the platform. Likes from very big accounts, let's say 1 million follower accounts, count as "powerlikes" and just a few of them are enough to boost your engagement rate through the roof. Engagement groups are trying to pretty much do the same thing but with a smaller scale, you usually have people within the same size of your account and this is why: The larger your account, the better engagement groups work. Also, a "Like" becomes less worth if the account is constantly liking many posts since it becomes evident that this account is not only liking posts that it genuinely wants to show appreciation for but rather as a strategy to get more exposure.

4.3 Create Your Own Engagement Group

The concept of engagement groups is fantastic and it can definitely help out your account, however there are very few engagement groups that are actually of high quality and it is nearly impossible to find the good ones unless you already know many people in that field. The solution is to create your own engagement groups where you can make sure that the quality of the participating accounts is of high quality and you can set your own rules. You can start creating groups on any platform you like, telegram is the most used one but DM groups on Instagram work as well. Another alternative is Discord, and although it is mostly used by gamers, it still offers a lot of customization options and great tools to moderate the chat rooms which can come handy when you start your own engagement groups.

How To Find Participants For Engagement Groups

You can find other members by searching through hashtags that are within the same niche as you. Go to the top hashtags and look for accounts that roughly have the same size, ideally a little larger than your own account so you get the maximum out of it. DM those accounts and ask them if they are interested in joining your engagement group, roughly tell them how it works and what the benefits for them are if they decide to join. This can be a time-consuming process but it is worth it since you will have the best possible quality that an engagement group can have. Another method is by using reddit and going through relevant subreddits. If the subreddits allow it then you can make your own topic where you look for people to join your groups, be sure to check the rules before you post otherwise your post might be taken down. Once you add members to your group try to build up relationships with them and bond in some sort of way. Most of the time you can get huge support from other people if you spend a little quality time chatting to them. Furthermore, this ensures that the members value your group and thus follow your rules.

4.4 Set Your Rules

The rules of your engagement groups are a vital part and will play a role of how well your engagement group will do when it comes to actually helping the members grow naturally with the use of the algorithm. Instagram has detected engagement groups and is actively working against their efficiency as it is in some way seen as "cheating the system" as people get an unfair advantage by artificially boosting up their engagement on new posts. Hence, in order for your engagement group to work you will need to make it as natural as possible. This means that the members should actually spend time following and liking each other, posting genuine comments and perhaps have some DM conversations before the engagement boosting starts. By doing this you deceive the Instagram algorithm, making it think that you actually are friends with each other so the upvoting and commenting on new posts is completely natural and not artificial anymore. As your rule #1 you should add that the members should never post a direct link to the new post that they want to have engagement on. If they post a direct link, the intentions of the likes will become obvious and they will not be of high quality. Instead, they should just link their profile and the other members manually go to the newest post and engage with it. Your rule #2 should be that no member posts more than once a day, this is important to prevent spammy behaviour. Another rule should include that the comments need to be genuine and not 1-2 word or emoji comments, those have no value, but make sure that everyone adds real and appropriate comments to the post. Additionally, you can add further rules if you want to, this is your group and you can individualize it depending on what you want to accomplish.

4.5 Conclusion Engagement Groups

Once the rules are established it is important that everyone is following those. Add a disclaimer that members need to report someone that is not following them as it will lower the quality significantly if you have people that do not take this seriously. Once again try to have a friendly and open environment and aim to become a community rather than just a group that likes and comments on each other's posts. This is a time-consuming process but if you do this correctly it can do wonders to your account and to your networking as you will have a lot of people that you can talk to and potentially collaborate with. Concluding, it is safe to say that engagement groups can work but they are time consuming and only worth it if you are a part of a high quality one. If you do not want to invest the time in finding or creating a high-quality engagement group, then it is advised to not join one at all as it will hurt your reach if it is a low-quality group.

5. Shoutouts

Shoutouts can be a great way of growing on Instagram too, there are different types of shoutouts and some are free while others require you to go into your pocket and pay a certain amount of money. The essence of a shoutout is that another account, preferably a bigger account than yours, posts one of your pictures in their story or in their feed and makes a call to action for their followers to go ahead and check out your account. This method can be helpful to grow your following and get high quality followers that are genuinely following you because they like your content. However, this method is less efficient and takes a lot of time or money (or both) to be really effective in growing your account. It can be categorized into two different sub methods which include paid shoutouts or shoutout for shoutout.

5.1 Detecting a Good Profile

In order to find good profiles that are worth the time and effort (and money), you will need to check the profiles beforehand and look out for things such as their comments. The comments are a great indicator to see if it is worth doing a shoutout for shoutout with another account, if the posts get a decent amount of likes but only very few comments then this shows that their followers are not investing a lot of time to properly engage with their posts. This means that they are highly unlikely to even read the post, they just tap a like and move on to the next post. Thus, stay away from accounts that have not a lot of real and genuine comments because they will not bring you any followers at all. As an example: I once did a shoutout for shoutout with an account that had 15.000 followers with a decent engagement rate. The comments were lackluster as they mostly were emojis or one-two word comments and I had my doubts, yet I still went through with it. The shoutout brought me a stunning 1 follower. In comparison, a shoutout from a

5.000 account once brought me 50 followers within one day so you should really not be worrying too much about the number of followers that an account has but focus more on the authenticity and the commitment of their followers.

5.2 Shoutout for Shoutout

A shoutout for shoutout is the free version of the shoutout growth method. Since you trade shoutouts with another account, this is less effective but saves you a lot of money in the process. Furthermore, you start to network with other people within your niche and potentially bond with them for future projects and collaborations. For a Shoutout for Shoutout to successfully work without being a waste of time you will need to have at least 1.000 followers so you can search for accounts within the same range and ask them if they are interested in doing shoutouts for shoutouts with you. Before you DM another account to ask them whether or not they are interested in doing a shoutout for shoutout, you will need to do sufficient research on their engagement rate and see if their followers are actually committed to their content. One easy way to do this is to check their average likes and comments.

Once you are sure that you want to do a shoutout for shoutout DM or email the person and pitch them your idea. This is like selling a product, you need to be original and convincing that both parties can benefit from this. Many people agree to do a 24-hour shoutout where they post a picture and add a caption that you can choose and tag you in their post (you do the same for them). After 24 hours you are both free to delete the post, however, many people leave the posts up if they got a good engagement on that post. After all, the more quality content the better.

5.3 Paid Shoutouts

Paid shoutouts are good if you have a budget and want to grow faster or if you do not want to do shoutouts in return. In general, paid shoutouts are the same as a shoutout for shoutout with the exception that you trade with money instead of a shoutout from your side. This, however, allows you to look for larger accounts that have more than 100.000 followers. Hence, their shoutouts will net you a lot more followers than the smaller accounts that you target in the shoutout for shoutout method. The price range varies a lot and it all comes down to the quality of the account that you want a shoutout from. Note: Stay away from websites that offer shoutouts for money, as 99.9% of the accounts on their websites have bot followers and fake engagement. If you want to get shoutouts you will need to personally approach accounts that have a lot of followers and check their authenticity first. Before you pay for a shoutout, follow the account and see if they are doing an unusual amount of shoutouts. Some accounts do 3 shoutouts per day, obviously you will not get much from an account that is spamming shoutouts as their followers will be numb towards new shoutouts. Be prepared to have rather high expenses if you decide to do paid shoutouts, a 24 hour shoutout from an account that has 100.000 followers costs around 100-500$ and it can bring you around 100-500 followers, the numbers can vary a lot. If you decide to go for this method, make sure that you only pick accounts with a very good engagement rate.

5.4 Conclusion Shoutouts

Shoutouts are like a surprise bag, you can never know what will come out of it even if you do enough research. One time you might be lucky and get 100 followers with one shoutout, the next time you might only get 5 even if the accounts were similar to each other and both looked good at first. It is extremely time consuming because you will have to DM every account and you will not get an answer or you will be rejected by most accounts that you message. However, it is important to not get demotivated from your misfortune as it is generally a really good and healthy way to grow naturally and ensure future growth. Additionally, you can combine shoutouts with engagement groups as you might find some people that you start bonding with after the initial exchange which is the key to success. Surround yourself with people who share the same interest and hopefully help you out in the future. If you do not want to use the Follow for Follow method, then the Shoutouts method is one of the best alternatives to get going on Instagram.

6. The Viral Comment Method

One of the lesser known methods is to post comments on new posts from very big accounts with the intention to make your comment go viral by quickly getting a lot of likes on the comment and thus attracting a lot of people towards your account. The viral comment method works great if you have a good sense of what the people like to read in the comment section of Instagram posts.

6.1 How it Works

For starters, you will once again need to find target accounts that are within your niche. This time, however, you want to be looking for the very big accounts that have at least more than 100.000, preferably even more than 1 Mio. followers. Bigger accounts bring a larger return of investment, which means that you can get more followers by commenting on an account with 10 Million followers rather than an account with 100.000 followers. The reason is simple, the bigger the account, the more people are going to see your viral comment. Nonetheless, it becomes harder to successfully post a viral comment on larger accounts, so it is recommended to try out different things and see what fits best for you. In order to find those accounts, you can search through the explore page, go to the hashtags and search through the top posts or you can use google to find blog posts that list the biggest accounts in a specific niche.

Once the target account is selected, you will need to turn on notifications for whenever the account makes a new post. Instagram conveniently offers that option and you will not be needing to get a third app to do so. Simply go to one of their posts and click the 3 dots on the top right. Afterwards click on "turn on post notifications". Once you do that, you will receive push notifications whenever the account makes a new post and you can then go over and quickly post a comment. It is very important that you are fast, since large accounts receive hundreds of comments within the first few minutes and you do not want your comment to get buried under the masses of comments that are already there. Ideally, you should make the comment within 1 minute of the post being up. While this might sound ambitious, it is crucial in making the viral comment method work because the timing is key in this method. Since the timing is very important, most people have pre-written comments that they comment with the help of shortcuts, so they do not lose any time and have an advantage over the others.

You might have noticed it yourself before too, many top comments under a celebrity's post are generic and not very original, yet they have thousands of likes and appear at the top spot of the comment section. Those people got there by making use of the viral comment method and their comments are copy-pasted from a previous comment more often than not. For the best success rates, it is best to do research beforehand, look at old posts and go through the comments to see which ones were the most successful ones. Every niche has their own tone and if you can find out which tone fits best for you and what type of structure the comment should have then you can go ahead and try your luck. But, it is important to mention that there will be many failed attempts to make comments go viral as there is a lot of competition and many people that are trying to do the same thing. Do not be discouraged, only a few successful viral comments can net you hundreds of followers. Just like fishing, you can improve your chances by learning the best strategy but in the end it all comes down to whether the fish is willing to bite or not.

6.2 Conclusion to The Viral Comment Method

The viral comment method is great because it can be used in every stage of your growth campaign even though it becomes significantly easier once you have more followers and build up an authority. With a little bit of practice and experience you can turn this method into a goldmine and quickly grow while gaining high quality followers that are within your niche and that are invested in your future content. Moreover, it is less time consuming than many other methods, but it is much more random with the results. If you are unfortunate, you might spend hours in trying to finally manage to make a comment go viral and never succeed or you are lucky and post one viral comment after the other. As a result, the growth rate with this method is not predictable but it is worth doing some testing and getting your feet wet.

7. Improve Your Engagement Rate

As mentioned before, the engagement rate is a crucial factor when it comes to Instagram growth as it will determine whether your posts will only be seen by your existing followers or be seen by other people outside of your follower base. If you keep your followers engaged with your content and create a good relationship with them, then this will pay off in the future of your Instagram career as it will enable you to rank in top hashtags and reach the explore page whenever you make a new post. Instagram's algorithm looks at the amount of people that have seen your post and compares it to the people that have taken an action such as liking, commenting, sharing, saving or even zooming into the picture. Once the percentage of people that engage with your post is high enough and you get plenty of likes, the algorithm will categorize your post as high quality since it sees that your post is good enough for most people to react to and share their affection to it. The previously mentioned engagement groups already help improving your engagement rate but there are more things you can do.

7.1 Do Not Post Too Often

Over the past years of my social media career I have read all sorts of gibberish, one of them was to post as often as you can. Some people even advised to post as much as 6 times a day because they said that more content is better. However, this is a huge mistake that can destroy your engagement rate and have a severely negative impact on the commitment of your followers. Furthermore, you will create a feeling of numbness that your followers will feel towards your new posts since they will not feel like you are posting anything special but that you are out there trying to shove content down their throats. Whenever you make a new post, it needs to be something special and something that your followers can look forward to. Thus, it is strongly advised to not post more than 1 or 2 times a day while it is possible to make exceptions to this if you plan on having something like an event where you want to make more posts.

7.2 Be Consistent

While it is important to not spam your followers, you will need to find a routine for your Instagram posts and actions. This does not mean that you absolutely have to post every day or even every second day, but it means that you need to make sure that you do not have longer periods of "dry phases" where you are not posting anything at all. The idea behind this is that you need your followers to be consistently engaging with your content, not only because they will be more likely to connect with you on a mental scale, but also because Instagram will recommend them your posts more the more they are in contact with you. In your Instagram feed, the posts are not randomly listed but undergo a very complex process that determines which post will be shown at the top of every individual feed. Instagram calculates which accounts are the closest to you by looking at things like engagement on posts, DMs, profile visits, zooming in pictures and average time spent looking at the account's posts. If you spend more time looking through one account's posts than you do on average, then Instagram will help you see more of the person's posts by ranking their posts higher on your feed which brings us to the next point. Furthermore, you can use schedulers like Hootsuite, which is a free website, to schedule posts in advance so you can have a small relief when it comes to posting consistently.

7.3 Engage with Your Followers

Because of Instagram's nature to rank posts based on individual preferences you will need to engage with your followers to higher the chances of your post to be seen by most of them. If you are in contact with many people on Instagram, this will be very helpful for your posts to be quickly seen by them. Many people on Instagram follow hundreds of other people so if you are just one of them, then your post might be buried under the posts of the other people and you will need to make sure that you work against that. By regularly and genuinely engaging with your followers you will build up relationships that will help you get seen more often by your own followers and this will boost up your engagement rate quite a lot. Even things such as simply leaving a comment on one of your follower's posts will make it likely that they will interact with your account in some way, they might answer your comment, like it or even visit your profile and look through it. This will make them much more likely to see your posts in the future since the algorithm will rank your posts higher the more they interact with you. Therefore, you should include engaging with your followers in your daily routine, it does not have to be too long but 15 minutes of liking and commenting on other people's posts can already boost your engagement rate.

7.4 Post Engaging Captions

Captions can be a nice way to persuade your followers to comment on your posts. It is an option for you to make a call to action or ask a question which will likely cause more interaction on your post. Instagram is a social media platform and should therefore be used as one. Do not post boring captions with no meaning, try to be creative and awaken the interest of your followers within the first sentence of your caption. Remember that most people scroll through hundreds of posts every day, so you need to catch your followers' interest quickly since they often only read superficially without paying a lot of attention to the actual things you want to express. Hence, keep it simple and concise to pull the people out of their scrolling on autopilot and into your world.

7.5 Remove Bot Followers

Lastly, it is advised to remove any bot followers that you might have gotten during the time on Instagram. This is not an accusation, this happens to everyone since there are millions of bots around that are randomly following accounts across the globe. However, the issue with bot followers is that they will raise your total amount of followers without ever engaging with your content. As a result, your engagement rate will automatically take a hit and those followers will not have any worth to you. You can mostly detect bots by weird usernames that make no sense, they often have no profile picture and if they do you can often detect them by looking at their profile since bots mostly only have less than 3 posts that are random.

8. The Correct use of Hashtags

Everybody on Instagram knows what hashtags are useful for, yet they are misunderstood most of the time. Yes, hashtags are a great way to bring traffic to your account page and they help you reach other people that are not following you, but most people use them in a wrong way. In order for hashtags to be effective and helpful to your growth it is important to do enough research and find the hashtags that are relevant but also right for the size of your account. Hashtags like #photography have thousands of posts every day so if you want to be seen by the people that search for this hashtag you will need to rank in the "top posts" of that hashtag and it becomes harder for the large hashtags that have millions of posts.

Websites like metahashtags.com (also free) can help a lot during the stages of research. Look through the hashtags and compare them to the size of your own account which will help you determine which hashtags to use. For example, an account that has 1.000 followers should not be using too many hashtags that have above 500.000 posts and should be focusing more on smaller hashtags that have less than 100.000 posts because the chances of ranking in the top posts will be significantly higher. Smaller hashtags can bring you a lot of traffic too so do not be discouraged, in fact, they will help you a lot more than the big hashtags until you have a high number of followers.

Instagram allows 30 hashtags per post and it is advised to at least use 25 with each post. If you already have a huge following, then hashtags will become less important and you can just post 1-3 or none because you will mostly reach out to other people via the explore page. However, for smaller accounts that have not reached the 100.000 followers mark yet, hashtags are a great way of reaching that goal. Additionally, you can use the triangle method for posting hashtags where you mostly use hashtags that have less than <100.000 posts as the foundation, then a few bigger ones that have between 500.000 and 1 Mio. posts and 2-3 huge ones that have more than 1 Mio. posts as shown in the example below.

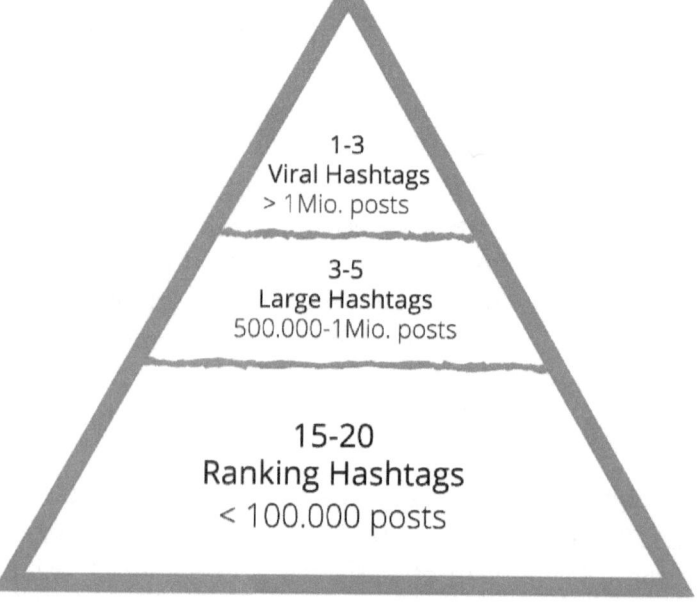

Depending on your size and your engagement you can play around with these numbers and do some testing to see what works the best. Viral hashtags have a huge competition and are therefore really hard and almost impossible to rank for smaller accounts, so you need to focus more on the realistic ones and play to your strength. It is not a bad idea to add a few, sometimes posts become viral even from smaller accounts and then you will be glad that you have a few viral hashtags in there since they will boost your numbers even further.

8.1 How to Do Hashtag Research

As already mentioned before, there are many tools that can help you out when you are doing your hashtag research. However, you will need to individually compile your hashtags for every post you make to get the most out of it. At first, you will need to think about what makes your picture special, using generic hashtags will not bring much value to your reach because your post will be buried under thousands of other posts and will be unlikely to be seen by the right people that are specifically interested in the content you have posted. Your foundation of hashtags should be consisting of hashtags that describe something special on your post by narrowing down the topic to target the right audience. Try to find hashtags that people are actively searching for. If you use #pics your posts have the chance to be seen by thousands of people but the chance of them actually being interested in your post particularly is very low. Therefore, it is best to find hashtags that have a committed audience, even if the audience is small. If 10 people see your post but they are specifically looking for golden retriever pictures you will have a higher chance of getting them to follow you than having 1.000 people see your post on #pics because the audience will be much more targeted and tailored towards the content that you post.

Since I talked so much about dogs, it would be unfair to leave you hanging without adding a picture of a golden boy!

(photo taken from wirestock)

In this example you post a picture of your dog in a park with a sunset in the background. During the first stage of research you can take the most obvious things of the photo and type them into the search bar in the hashtag search option in order to see what other hashtags you can find that are not as large.

Q goldenretriever	⊘ Cancel	Q photography	⊘ Cancel	Q sunset	⊘ Cancel
Top Accounts **Tags** Places		Top Accounts **Tags** Places		Top Accounts **Tags** Places	

#	#goldenretriever 24.8m posts	#	#photography 659m posts	#	#sunset 266m posts
#	#goldenretrieversofinstagram 4.7m posts	#	#photographylovers 21.3m posts	#	#sunsetlover 5m posts
#	#goldenretrieverpuppy 4.2m posts	#	#photographyart 4.4m posts	#	#sunsetphotography 6.3m posts
#	#goldenretrievers 3.5m posts	#	#photography___ 3.3m posts	#	#sunsetlovers 8.6m posts
#	#goldenretrieverlove 1.5m posts	#	#photographylover 9.4m posts	#	#sunsets 16.3m posts
#	#goldenretrievertoday 594k posts	#	#photographyeveryday 9.7m posts	#	#sunset_pics 6.5m posts
#	#goldenretrieverpuppies 637k posts	#	#photographylife 4.5m posts	#	#sunset_vision 7.9m posts
#	#goldenretrieverofinstagram 496k posts	#	#photographysouls 9.3m posts	#	#sunsetporn 4.2m posts
#	#goldenretrieverlovers 844k posts	#	#photographyislife 11m posts	#	#sunsets_captures 823k posts
#	#goldenretrieverworld 941k posts	#	#photographyaddict 1.5m posts	#	#sunsets_oftheworld 800k posts

The main hashtags in this picture would be #sunset, #photograpgy, #goldenretriever, #dog, #park. Once you type on of these in the search bar you will see that there are a lot of hashtags recommended that contain the word you typed in and add something to it. If you type in #goldenretriever and scroll down you will be able to find smaller hashtags that you will have a better chance ranking in and that have a committed audience. You can use the pyramid schematic from above to help you decide which hashtags to choose and in which quantity. Think about which hashtags are likely to be searched or even by people to get the highest chance of success. You can mix the words up or change them a little to find more related hashtags and get new ideas. If you like one of the hashtags, make sure to note it down and assign it to the correct scale so you can quickly see how many ranking hashtags you have. Below you can find an example of hashtags that would be fitting for the image of the dog with a sunset.

Ranking Hashtags:
#ig_dogs (93K), #autumnsunset (93K), #sunsetcaptures (96K), #doggyfriends (97K), #goldenretrieveroninstagram (65K), #goldenretrievergram (100K), #goldenretrieverinstagram (74K),

#goldenretrieversarethebest (80K), #goldenretrievernation (54K), #goldenretrieverhype (65K), #goldenretrievercommunity (11K), #dogphotographylife (49K), #sunsetcaptures (96K), #sunsetdog (23K), #sunset_pic (47K), #sunset_shot (49K), #sunsetwalks (50K), igsunsets (50K)

Large Hashtags:
#igsunset (720K), #sunset_lovers (800K), #sunsets_captures (823K), #sunset_love (852K), #sunsetpics (494K), #goldenretrieverworld (941K), #goldenretrieverlovers (844K), #goldenretrieversworld (835K), #goldenretrieverpuppies (637K), #goldenretrieverclub (537K)

Viral Hashtags:
#goldenretriever (24.4M), #goldenretrieverlove (1,5M)

With this selection we have added 30 high quality hashtags that are all related to the picture and are therefore going to attract people that are targeted directly around the picture. It is very important that you make sure to have relevant hashtags because even if you get a high exposure, it will not help you out if you cannot transform it into followers for your page. A wrongly used hashtag is going to be completely useless, since the audience that is searching for that hashtag is not going to be interested in your post as they have searched for something specific and if your post does not match that, they will simply scroll past it and maybe even report you for using a wrong hashtag. Imagine going to a pizza place and being fully committed to eat that delicous pizza you have been dreaming of for the past 5 days. If someone were to offer you something completely different, let us say a car dealer comes up and wants to sell you a car, you will be very unlikely to pay him any attention as you will not simply abandon your pizza in order to buy something that you were not looking for in the first place. Despite the fact that you are hungry for pizza. Now that you understood the fundamentals aboud hashtags it is time to get to the next point.

8.2 Create Your Own Hashtag

Next up is a tip that is used very rarely but has a lot of potential. Creating your own hashtag can help out a lot with your branding but it is obviously difficult to do if you do not already have a big following that joins your trend. Creating a hashtag needs to be viewed as a rather metaphorical than technical method since you are not really creating something new but rather start making a hashtag be associated with your own brand or account. This means that you choose a hashtag that is preferably not used so far and start putting effort into making people associate the specific hashtag with your account. Some profiles already use this method, they tell their followers to use a certain hashtag and tag them in their posts for a chance to be featured on the big account's profile. This is a great way for having other people advertise your account without even doing the work yourself once everything is properly set up. However, establishing the hashtag and getting other people to use it can be rather tricky for smaller accounts. There definitely needs to be an incentive that is good enough for using your hashtag otherwise you will not find enough people who are willing to use your hashtag. The incentives can vary a lot such as shoutouts, giveaways, story features etc. you can be creative with this one. There are also niche-specific things like #drawthisinyourstyle where artists draw an existing character in their own style and tag the original artist in their post. There are different things in every niche so keep an eye out for them and try to utilize them for your growth.

9. Account Trust Score

While it is not officially confirmed, every account on Instagram undoubtedly has an individual "trust score" which is put together by different variables and it mostly represents the integrity of your account. There are certain things you need to consider making sure that your account trust score does not become negative, as it can have severe consequences if you are not careful with your behaviour on Instagram. As mentioned before, there are a lot of bots around and Instagram came up with a system to rank users based on the authenticity of their actions within the app/website. If they notice too much spammy or unnatural behaviour they will limit your reach and stop you from reaching many people with your posts. You might end up with action blocks, shadow bans or a complete ban if you use unconventional methods such as using bots to automate the Follow/Unfollow method. Shadow bans will limit your reach and you will not be able to rank in hashtags. Here are some things to consider when you look at account trust scores:

Account Age

Firstly, your account age plays a big role in having an authentic account. During the first 14 days, your account will be very vulnerable to negative consequences, so it is advised to be careful and tame with your actions such as DMs, comments, likes and follows. Be sure to warm up the account properly without spamming too much as you will quickly get blocked from doing further actions.

Spam Protection

Once your account has been warmed up properly and exists for more than two weeks you can be more generous with your likes and other actions. However, whatever you do, it needs to be natural human behaviour. This means that you should never follow 100 people in the span of 10 minutes, nobody does that and it becomes obvious that you are trying to get other people to follow you as quickly as possible. This is where Instagram's spam protection will intervene and you will receive blocks from further following others.

Valid Email

Connecting your Instagram account to a valid Email of a good provider is crucial to gain Instagram's trust. If you sign up with a throwaway Email from a shady provider without even confirming the Email as yours then you will have a harder time getting your trust score to be good enough for you to live a carefree life on Instagram.

Affiliate Links
Affiliate links are a good way for you to earn a little extra money, however, they are also a good indicator for spam accounts that have the only one intention of earning money by getting other people to buy their products. While affiliate links can harm your account, you do not have to be concerned too much if it comes from a trusted source and you do not change it too often.

Reports
Getting often reported on Instagram can have a largely negative impact on your account. It is a clear indication that something with your account is wrong since many people report you to Instagram. If this happens too often, it might hurt your account beyond repair, so you need to be very careful to not spam other users, have no inappropriate content and behave like a human being.

Changing IP Location Often
Changing IPs is to some extent normal behaviour and you will not be punished for it. Even when you fly to other countries for your vacation you will not have to worry about negative impacts on your Instagram account. The issue will occur when the location from where you access Instagram changes too much in a short period of time. This happens when you use proxies or VPNs, if you give your Instagram account details to other people or if your account gets hacked. As a result, to protect your account, Instagram will either block your account, ask for Email or Phone verification or ban your account if this happens repeatedly.

Avoid Banned Hashtags

There are some hashtags that are banned on Instagram, they mostly consist of hashtags that happen to have explicit or adult content. In order to prevent Instagram's users from those pictures, some hashtags do not show the "recent posts", instead you can find a text saying that the hashtag is banned. For example #sunbathing:

<   **#sunbathing**   ...

Recent posts from #sunbathing are currently hidden because the community has reported some content that may not meet Instagram's community guidelines

Learn More

If you use one of those hashtags your trust score might take a hit and your post will be shadowbanned across all hashtags. Therefore, you should be careful with the hashtags you want to use, otherwise they will severely limit your reach. You can identify banned hashtags by individually checking them which is very time consuming, or you can find a complete list of banned hashtags on metahashtags.com/banned-hashtags/ or similar pages on the internet.

Bot Followers
If you decide that you do not care about your engagement rate and only want to show off to your friends that you have so many followers, your account might also end up being punished as a result. If you realize that you have been getting more and more bot followers, make sure to block them so they cannot do any further harm to your account and by doing that you will also improve your engagement rate. Sometimes people fall victim to bot followers, where an agency is trying to convince a potential client that they are great at providing followers quickly. If you notice this on your own account, change your username and block all the

bot accounts. By changing your username, the link to your profile will also change and the bots will therefore land on an empty page.

9.1 What Happens if Your Account Trust Score is Bad?

Precisely, if your trust score is bad then your account will be very vulnerable to action blocks. This means that even after just liking 10 pictures in a natural way you might end up receiving a block where you will not be able to do any further actions for 24 hours, 7 days or even 2 weeks. Furthermore, you are in risk of being shadowbanned which will result in your post being seen by far less people than usual, you will not show up in hashtags and even your likes and comments might not be visible to other users. For you, everything will seem normal as you will be able to see your comments and posts, however, they will be invisible for other users. Furthermore, your reach will be trimmed and you will not be able to spread your work out to as many people as before. Eventually, if you keep making actions that hurt your account trust score, your account will be banned permanently and you will lose everything you have worked for. Hence, make sure that you act naturally and keep the daily limits in mind.

10. Use Other Social Media Platforms (Reddit)

This is my biggest tip of them all, using other social media platforms is vital to an organic and natural growth on Instagram. Other platforms like YouTube or Reddit are exceptional for reaching other people that have not followed you before. Those are perfect for reaching an audience without the necessity of having a big following before. YouTube and Reddit provide great discoverability as long as the content you post in there is interesting enough to be seen. Thanks to their great discoverability, they perfect for reaching an audience without the necessity of having a big following before. YouTube is a little bit more time intensive since you will need to create, cut and edit videos to upload on the platform. On Reddit, however, you can post content without having to put too much effort into it. Neat infographics, interesting facts about your business or funny pictures are great material that does not need much time to produce. Reddit is often called "the frontpage of the internet" because it has millions of daily users and it has a niche for almost everyone and everything. It is perfect if you are an individual that creates their own content because you will be able to post it for millions of people to see. The only limit to your success is the quality of the content that you produce. If you are a photographer and you can take high quality and beautiful pictures, then you will certainly be able to reach a very large number of people by just posting it in one of the dedicated subreddits. If the people on there like your content, they will upvote it and the post will reach the front page which will skyrocket the views on your picture. Now you might ask, how is this going to help you out getting more Instagram followers? You can simply link your Instagram profile in the comments in almost every subreddit! Because Reddit can be confusing for many people that do not have a lot of experience with it, I will explain the process of converting Redditors (this is what people on Reddit are called) into your followers on Instagram.

10.1 Finding the Right Subreddit

Reddit is divided into subreddits that all cover a specific niche, there are subreddits for memes, food, recipes, photography, video games, sports, etc. Subreddits are distinguished with the /r/ in front of their name and they are community driven, which means that the community controls the posts by upvoting or downvoting content depending on whether they like it or not. There are huge subreddits like /r/pics that includes anything that is a picture with more than 25 million subscribed users or /r/earthporn where you can post pictures of our beautiful earth with more than 20 million subscribed users. As mentioned above, you can find a subreddit about almost anything where you can share your work. In order to find the fitting subreddits you can simply google "reddit + your niche" and the fitting subreddits will most often be in the search results.

10.2 Get Yourself Familiar with The Rules

While Reddit has sitewide rules, every subreddit has additional rules that need to be individually taken into account when you want to make a post over there. For example, /r/pics does not allow direct links to any social media page in the comments but you are allowed to add your Instagram handle (i.e. @Michael_Kalamaris) and let the people know that you have an Instagram account where you post more content. Admittedly, this is not the most elegant solution, but it works. However, there are more lenient subreddits like /r/earthporn that allow you to add a hyperlink to your Instagram profile in the comment section so that the users only have to click once to get to your profile which is much more convenient and will get you better results. Therefore, it is important to know about the rules so you avoid any infractions which can lead to a ban in that subreddit if you repeatedly break the rules.

10.3 Things to Consider When Posting

Reddit is a very special place, the users are tech-savvy and they are not easily fooled when it comes to advertisement or posting content with the only intention to self-promote. Thus, whenever you make a post, do not be obvious with your intention and put in some effort to make your post a genuine contribution to the subreddit. If you make a post it will first be shown in the "new" tap of the subreddit. Hence, make sure that it is high quality and original so you can get upvotes which will bring you to the "hot" page of the subreddit. Moreover, most people on Reddit are browsing through the "hot" section and will therefore not even see your post as it will be buried under new posts and never see the light of day. With this in mind, it is crucial to gain upvotes which will push your post to the desired "hot" page and depending on the size of the subreddit you can reach thousands or millions of people just with that. Additionally, if your post does exceptionally well, you have the chance to reach the /r/all page of reddit, where the very best posts of all the subreddits are merged together and they can be seen by every Redditor on the platform. Most of the time, however, reaching the top spot of the "hot" page of a bigger subreddit can bring you hundreds of followers, while even smaller ones can net you enough for a steady growth. To provide some numbers, one of my posts on /r/earhporn received more than 2.000 upvotes which made it be seen by a lot of users and it brought me around 120 followers, I created that post within 5 minutes. It is also important to note that these numbers are not impossible to achieve, if you have the right content for a subreddit and the content is good, then you can easily reach those numbers and even surpass them.

Another thing to consider is that your Reddit account needs to have a good amount of "Karma" in order to post in most subreddits. This amount is not disclosed to prevent bots but it is mostly around 25 Karma in order to not get your posts shadowbanned. Karma essentially is Reddit appreciation score, if you gain upvotes on comments or posts then your overall Karma will rise and you will be able to brag about your insane Karma. However, other than bragging rights and the authenticity that your account gains with it, there is nothing you can do with Karma so all you need to know is: if you have a fresh account on Reddit you need to contribute and comment on other posts until you get enough upvotes to be able to post in most subreddits.

10.4 Conclusion on Social Media Platforms (Reddit)

Because of the fact that Instagram itself is not really good at helping users grow their accounts without working too hard, it is great to use the help of other social media platforms that are great at distributing your content to the world. It is clever to make use of them and since you usually already have a lot of content that you posted on Instagram, you can reuse this content and put it on Reddit. It is not very time consuming and it can give you a huge number of engaged followers that love your content and want to support you on your way to grow your account even further. Once you get yourself familiar, it basically becomes a piece of cake, and let us be honest, who does not like cake? After all, there are so many kinds of cake that there is something in it for everyone.

11. Summing Up

Since there has been a lot of information to process, I will provide an infographic with all the characteristics in one view:

	Difficulty	Time intensive	Follower Requirements	effectiveness
Engaging With People (Follow for Follow)	Easy	High	None	High
Engagement Groups	Medium	High	High	Medium
Shoutout For Shoutout	Hard	High	High	Medium
Paid Shoutouts	Medium	Medium	None	Medium
Viral Comment Method	Hard	Medium	None	Low
Hashtag Use	Easy	Low	High	Medium
Other Social Media (Reddit)	Medium	Low	None	High

The "difficulty" shows how hard it is to successfully use the method. "Time intensive" shows how much time you will need to spend exercising this method. "Follower Requirements" shows how many followers you will need in order for this method to be working. Remember that you need a certain number of followers for some methods to work. Lastly, "effectiveness" shows how effective the method is in gaining new followers.

    In summary, growing on Instagram can be very difficult and time intensive especially if you do not know what you are doing. You will need to put in a lot of work to gain followers that will engage with your content. The methods explained in this book will hopefully provide enough guidance for you to have a precise idea of what you need to do in order to grow your account. Ideally, you will find the methods that work best for you and shape them with your personal touch depending on your individual needs. The methods provided can be adjusted and modified, try out different things and see what works best for your account since every niche has its own challenges and hurdles that you need to overcome. Furthermore, as you are now able to distinguish a good Instagram profile from a bad one, you will know what you need to be looking out for when it comes to your personal growth. The number of followers means nothing if your followers are not active and if they do not care about the content that you post. I believe that once you understand the system, you will be able to grow an account unlimitedly if you put enough time and effort into it. The first stage of Instagram growth is not a sprint, it is a marathon that needs a steady input of energy in order to reach for the stars. Once you get an account large enough, you will not have to be worrying too much about growing the account but more about having high quality content and earning money. Be prepared, create your own strategy and review your experience in order to find out what works best.

12. Did You Enjoy Reading This Book?

If you enjoyed reading this book but want to get even more out of your social media journey you can schedule a consulting meeting with me where we can discuss all sorts of questions that you have. Additionally, if you like the methods but you do not have enough time to work on your Instagram account you can sign me as your social media manager. Simply send an Email to Michael.Kouiroukidis@web.de and we can talk about the details. You can follow my personal account on Instagram @michael_kalamaris. Thank you for purchasing my book, I hope that this purchase was valuable to you. I would appreciate it if you rate my book and give me your honest opinion about the things you liked and the things that can be improved (link for the review https://www.amazon.com/dp/B08HY4B191). Have a good time growing your Instagram account!

www.ingramcontent.com/pod-product-compliance
Lightning Source LLC
Chambersburg PA
CBHW031554210526
45464CB00003B/1300